WONDERS OF THE NIGHT SKY

Project Book

Learn how to stargaze like the pros.

5 projects inside

INTRODUCTION

Welcome to the wonderful world of Stargazing.

This kit has been specifically designed for adults only.

Learning a new skill is always exciting - we're here to help you get started. In this booklet we want to show you how you can have fun whilst learning about the night sky. From the Art of Stargazing, Legends of the past, Marvels of the Universe and much more, this booklet will really open your eyes to the wonderful space around us.

Test your knowledge with quizzes, word searches and crosswords, while strengthening your stargazing skills by using our journal templates and Moon journal to track your progress as well as the phases of the Moon.

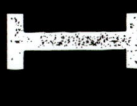

KIT CONTENTS

WHAT'S INCLUDED:
- Star Wheel
- Constellation poster
- Activity booklet

WHAT YOU'LL NEED:
- Binoculars/ Telescope (optional)
- Pen

SPACE
JOURNEY
Night Sky
CONSTELLATIONS
SOUTHERN HEMISPHERE
USA

TIPS & TECHNIQUES:

Block the Light!

- In the dark, you can see the most light! - Sounds weird right? Find an area that has as little light pollution as possible. If you want to use a light, use a red light as this will not impede your stargazing.

- Your eyes take about twenty minutes to adjust to the light (or lack of it!), so don't worry, it will all become clear.

- You do not need binoculars or telescopes, but they do come in handy for fainter stars, and for seeing much more detail, especially on the moon.

- Try stargazing at different times of the night and year for different results.

- One of the most common constellations you can see during the winter months in the UK is Orion's belt.

So, grab some warm clothes, a hot drink, journal and your STAR WHEEL (obviously), and let's go!

Weather

Winter is a better time to see the stars, than summer. (It's just a bit chilly!)

'Seeing' is better late at night and more difficult in the early evening.

It's best to Stargaze on a clear night. No clouds or rain.

'Transparency' is also important. This relates to the amount of dust, moisture, smoke, humidity as well as other types of pollution in the atmosphere.
This means the stability of the atmosphere, due to turbulence, affects how you see objects.
Poor 'seeing' conditions cause objects to appear blurry or moving when they aren't.

A STAR IS BORN!
What is a star?

Stars are bodies of gas (hydrogen and helium) that are scattered throughout our galaxy. They start off as dust and gas which can cause turbulence. When this happens, the clouds start to collapse due to the gravitational pull. This causes heat in the centre, creating what's known as a Protostar which eventually becomes a star as we know it! Their centre is so densely packed with hydrogen and helium that they cause a nuclear fusion reaction. This is when the nuclei of two atoms combine to make a new atom.

Types of star

The North Star

The North Star, or Polaris, is located on the tail of the constellation Ursa Minor. You can use the Star Wheel to help you find it.

Shooting Star

A shooting star is not actually a star. (I know, confusing right?) It is instead, a meteoroid that has entered our atmosphere (which then becomes a meteor), and starts burning up causing streaks of light. Sometimes, you will see something similar far in the distance and think, 'Hey, that looks like a shooting star!' This is probably a comet. Shooting stars are heading for Earth – comets are orbiting the sun.

Hot Blue Stars

Hot blue stars are bigger and hotter than our Sun, but tend to die after a few million years. These can be seen from Earth.

White Dwarfs

White dwarfs are the result of normal stars collapsing. This happens when they exhaust all their fuel. If this happens to a star that is part of a star system, they may pull matter from a neighbouring star adding it to its own surface. When this becomes too much it will result in a nova outburst.

Neutron Stars or Black Holes

If a star is over eight solar masses (one solar mass is approximately one of our suns), it is believed it will eventually end in a supernova! This is when, unlike a nova, the core explodes rather than the surface. This will end in either a Black hole or a neutron star.

Red Dwarf Stars

These stars are smaller than our Sun and are not as hot. This means they are more dim, but last a lot longer.

Red Giant Stars

Giant red stars are dying stars. They burn hydrogen outside their core. This results in the star swelling and becoming very bright. So bright that, just like the hot blue stars, they can be seen from Earth. This will eventually happen to our Sun, (but not for about five billion years yet, so don't worry we have a bit of time)!

The Sun

Our Sun is a star known as a yellow dwarf. It sits in the centre of our solar system and holds everything together with its gravitational pull. Although the Sun is a star - **do NOT look directly at it!**

STAR WHEEL

10

STAR WHEEL

Discover a whole new world with the 'Wonders of the Night Sky' star wheel.

HOW TO USE

Line the date......

1. Using a compass, face in a northerly direction and turn the star wheel until you find the point around its edge where today's date is marked on the rim of the circular disk. Align this with the current time. This should display all the constellations in the night sky.

....with the time.

2. Hold the star wheel up to the sky. The stars at the bottom half of the viewing window should match those you see above you in the sky. Constellations higher in the sky are closer to the centre of the map.

Find these stars!

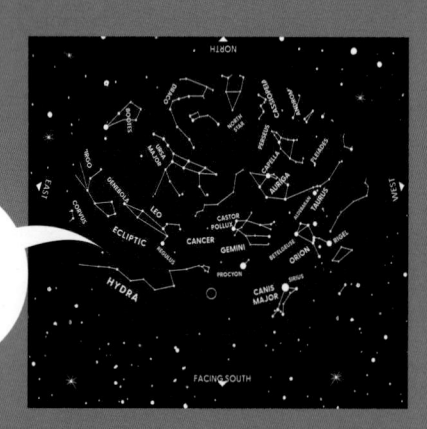

3. To see more, rotate the star wheel either facing East or West. The viewing window should match those you see above you in the sky.

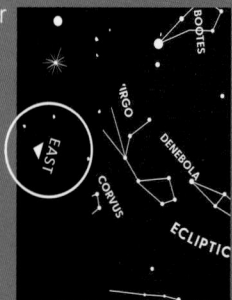

CAN YOU FIND?

1. THE BIG DIPPER/URSA MAJOR

The Big Dipper forms part of the constellation Ursa Major and is one of the easiest to identify in the sky.

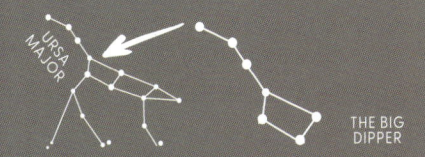

URSA MAJOR

THE BIG DIPPER

2. THE LITTLE DIPPER/URSA MINOR

The Little Dipper is part of the constellation Ursa Minor. Locate the top right star on the corner of the Big Dippers bucket and look north. Here, you will see Polaris, the North Star! Polaris represents the handle of the Little Dipper.

THE LITTLE DIPPER

3. ORION AND HIS BELT

Orion's Belt is formed by three main bright stars; Alnilam, Mintaka and Alnitak.

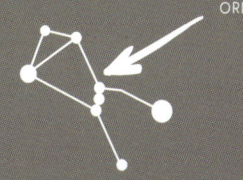

ORION'S BELT

Remember your Journal!

4. PLANETS

Five planets can be seen from Earth with the naked eye.
Mercury, Venus, Mars, Jupiter and Saturn! Venus is the brightest and is the first object to be seen in the evening. It is also the last to disappear before morning, earning it the names 'Evening' and 'Morning' star, (even though it isn't a star).

CONSTELLATIONS

What is a constellation?

A constellation is a group of stars that, together, form a recognisable form and are usually given a name to represent it.

Southern Hemisphere

CENTAURUS - Represented as a Centaur
LIBRA - Latin for 'weighing scales'
LUPUS - Latin for 'wolf'
CRUX - Latin for 'cross' - named for its cross-like shape
ANTARES - Scorpius, also known as 'Alpha Scorpii' and is also a red supergiant star!
HYDRA - The 'water snake' is the largest constellation in the sky
HADAR - Also known as 'Beta Centauri'
SAGITTARIUS - Latin for 'the archer'
CAPRICORNUS - Latin for 'horned goat'
PISCIS AUSTRINUS - Latin for 'southern fish'
FOMALHAUT - Hot blue star, and the brightest star, in the constellation 'Piscis Austrinus'
AQUARIUS - Known as 'Water-Bearer'
DENEB KAITOS - Is the brightest star in the constellation Cetus
MIRA - Is a red giant star
RIGEL - Is a blue supergiant star and the brightest star in the constellation of Orion
SIRIUS - Known as 'Dog Star' and is part of the constellation 'Canis Major' and is the brightest star in the sky!

Northern Hemisphere

LEO - Latin for 'lion'
REGULUS - Is the brightest star in the constellation Leo and a multiple star system
URSA MAJOR - Known as 'Great Bear'
DRACO - Latin for 'dragon'
URSA MINOR - Known as 'Little Bear'
CANCER - Latin for 'crab'
POLARIS - Known as the North Star and is part of the Ursa Minor constellation
GEMINI - Latin for 'twins'
ORION - Known as 'The Hunter'
BETELGEUSE - Is a red supergiant star and the second brightest star in the constellation Orion
ARIES - Latin for 'ram'
ANDROMEDA - Named after the daughter of Cassiopeia, in the Greek myth and is best known for the Andromeda Galaxy
TAURUS - Latin for 'bull'

DOT TO DOT CONSTELLATIONS

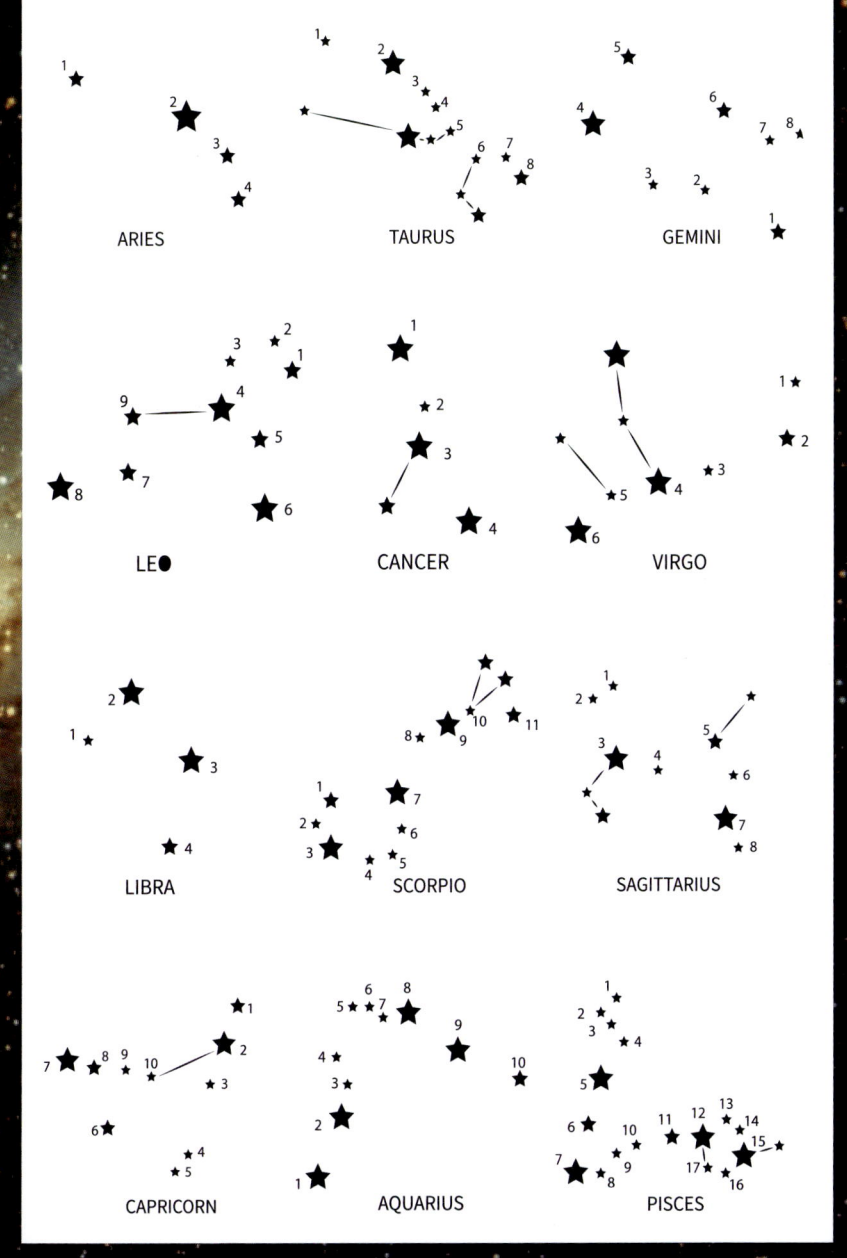

ARIES

TAURUS

GEMINI

LEO

CANCER

VIRGO

LIBRA

SCORPIO

SAGITTARIUS

CAPRICORN

AQUARIUS

PISCES

I'm named after American astronomer, Edwin Hubble!

LEGENDS

16

LEGENDS

Welcome to the past (And present!).
Read about the legends that shaped our knowledge and understanding of our wonderful universe, as well as current legends that are continuing their work.

LEGENDS

GALILEO GALILEI
(1564 – 1642)

"The father of modern science."
Galileo Galilei was a man of many talents. He was an Italian astronomer, engineer, polymath, mathematician and physicist and hailed from the city of Pisa. He is often credited with the creation of the optical telescope. In fact, Galileo actually improved on an existing telescope produced in another part of Europe.
He did, however, create a telescope later that could magnify objects twenty times. This allowed him to be the first person to observe and describe the moons of Jupiter, the rings of Saturn, the phases of Venus, as well as sunspots and the lunar surface.

CHRISTIAAN HUYGENS
(1629 – 1695)

Christiaan Huygens was a Dutch scientist who discovered the wave theory of light. He also, like Cassini and Galileo, made improvements to the telescope which allowed him to discover the true shape of Saturn's rings. Huygens also discovered Titan, Saturn's largest moon, marked the first moon spotted around the planet. He made the first known drawing of the Orion Nebula - a diffuse nebula in the Milky Way, south of Orion's Belt. Huygens recently had a probe named after him, which parachuted on Titan in 2005.

SIR ISAAC NEWTON
(1643 – 1727)

English astronomer famous for his work on forces, mainly gravity.
Newton is quoted as saying, 'If I have seen further, it is by standing upon the shoulders of giants'.
He calculated three laws describing the motion of forces between objects, known today as Newton's laws - the basic principles of modern physics. Known as one of the most influential figure's in all of science, Newton invented calculus, as well as investigating optics, mechanics, theology, experimental chemistry, and alchemy. The unit for force was named after him, the Newton (N).

HENRIETTA SWAN LEAVITT
(1868 – 1921)

Henrietta was one of several women working as a human 'computer' at Harvard College, identifying images of variable stars on photographic plates.
She discovered the 'period-luminosity relationship'. This is the connection between the brightness of a star and the time it takes for a star to go from bright to faint. This was known as the Cepheid variable which helped measure the distance of stars.
This relationship allowed astronomers, such as Hubble, to calculate the distance of stars and galaxies, the size of the Milky Way and the expansion of the universe.

ANNIE JUMP CANNON
(1863 – 1941)

"Census taker of the sky"
Cannon was an American astronomer who changed the way astronomers classify stars. She personally classified around 350,000 stars manually and created the Harvard spectral system, which is still used to classify stars today.
Stars used to be classified alphabetically from A to Q based on their temperatures. Annie realized, however, that a star creates different wavelengths which determine its colour. In 1901, she had improved the system with ten categories that used star's colour and brightness to classify.
Annie Jump Cannon inspired women to work in astronomy, a predominantly male industry.

LEGENDS

ALBERT EINSTEIN
(1879 – 1955)

German physicist Einstein became one of the most famous scientists in the early 20th century, best known for developing the theory of relativity. This theory is split into two categories, special and general.
The renowned physicist proposed a way of looking at the universe that went beyond current understanding. Einstein suggested that the laws of physics are the same throughout the universe. Space and time are in fact, connected creating space-time. Suggesting that events that occur at one time for one person could occur at a different time for another.

EDWIN HUBBLE
(1899 – 1953)

Edwin Hubble was an American astronomer who noticed a small blob in the sky outside of the Milky Way. Hubble discovered that the universe itself was expanding, this became known as Hubble's law. He proved that objects previously thought to be clouds of dust and gas, known as 'nebulae', were actually galaxies beyond the Milky Way.

CARL SAGAN
(1934 – 1996)

American astronomer Carl Sagan not only made important scientific studies in the fields of planetary science, he also managed to popularize astronomy. He authored over 600 scientific papers and wrote over 20 books about astronomy and natural sciences. Carl Sagan helped advise NASA on many missions to Venus, Mars, and Jupiter.
He was also a director and professor at Cornell Unversity!

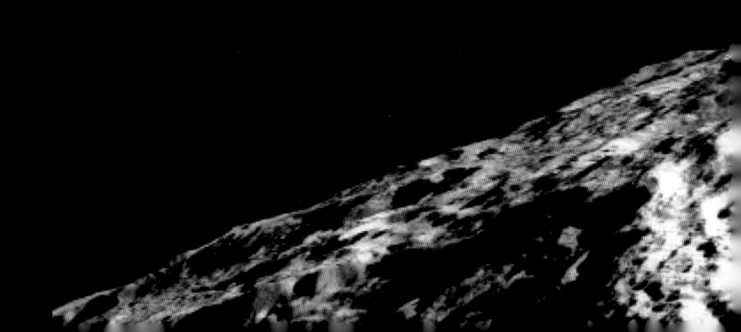

STEPHEN HAWKING
(1942 – 2018)

An English cosmologist, theoretical physicist and author, Hawking was considered one of the greatest scientific minds since Einstein. Although he suffered from motor neurone disease from the age of 20, Hawking managed to complete his doctorate in cosmology at Cambridge.
He proposed that there will be an end to the universe just as there was a beginning, and that there are no borders or boundaries. Hawking predicted that black holes emit radiation, known as Hawking radiation.

BRIAN COX
(born 3 March 1968)

Brian Cox is an English physicist and professor of particle physics at the School of Physics and Astronomy, Manchester, as well as The Royal Society Professor for Public Engagement in Science. He is also a presenter of many science programs for the BBC and radio including, **In Einstein's Shadow** and **Horizons**. Cox has also published works such as **Wonders of the Universe** and **Why does E=mc2?** with Jeff Forshaw.
Cox has won many awards for his work with science including the **British Association's Lord Kelvin Award**, **OBE 2010**, the **President's Medal**, and the **Royal Society Michael Faraday Prize** in 2012. He also tours giving talks about science all over the world!

WORDSEARCH

H	N	O	N	N	A	C
A	B	J	C	K	F	O
W	N	G	X	O	M	H
K	I	A	Q	S	X	U
I	E	L	S	N	N	B
N	T	I	A	E	O	B
G	S	L	G	G	T	L
O	N	E	A	Y	W	E
L	I	I	N	U	E	O
M	E	C	N	H	N	S
L	E	A	V	I	T	T

COX
EINSTEIN
HUBBLE
SAGAN
LEAVITT
HAWKING
GALILEI
HUYGENS
NEWTON
CANNON

23

ASTRONAUTS

24

Follow in the footsteps of the great men and women who have braved the unknown!
Find out who they are here!

ASTRONAUTS

YURI ALEKSEYEVICH GAGARIN
(9 March 1934 – 27 March 1968)

A Soviet pilot and cosmonaut, Gagarin completed one orbit of Earth on the 12th April 1961 speaking the first words ever spoken in space.

"I see Earth. It's so beautiful!"

Gagarin undertook a 108-minute spaceflight that reached an altitude of 203 miles (327 kilometres). Gagarin was the first human in space!

NEIL ALDIN ARMSTRONG
(August 5th 1930 – August 25th 2012)

On July 20th 1969 American astronaut, Neil Armstrong took the very first steps onto the grey, dusty surface of the moon. He spoke the famous line. "That's one small step for man, one giant leap for mankind."
This was the first moon landing! Twenty minutes later, Buzz Aldrin joined Armstrong on the surface where they gathered important data and planted a U.S flag.

VALENTINA VLADIMIROVNA TERESHKOVA
(born March 6th 1937)

Dr Valentina Tereshkova was the first and youngest female to go into space. Early in 1963, at age 26, she flew a single flight on Vostok 6 that logged more hours than all the Mercury astronauts, spending almost three days orbiting the Earth forty eight times.
In those three days, Tereshkova conducted science experiments to learn about the effects of space on the human body.

British chemist and astronaut, Helen Patricia Sharman was the first British person in space! Not only that, she was the first woman to visit the Mir space station.

Known as 'the Girl from Mars', Sharman applied to be an astronaut after hearing about vacancies on the radio in 1989. She competed against 13,000 other applicants. This resulted in her leaving her position as a chemist with the chocolate brand Mars.

The project she joined was known as Project Juno.

Eight years following Juno, Sharman wrote an autobiography entitled '**Seize the Moment**', as well as a children's book - '**The Space Place**'. Helen also presented radio and television programmes like BBC Schools.

From 2011, Helen worked as the group leader at the National Physical Laboratory of the Surface and Nano Analysis Group.

MAJOR TIMOTHY NIGEL PEAKE
(born 7th April 1972)

British Army Air Corps officer and European Space Agency astronaut, Major Timothy Nigel Peake was the first British astronaut to go aboard the International Space Station. On the 15th of January, he was the first British astronaut to do a spacewalk. During the London marathon, Tim ran on a treadmill the equivalent distance, completing it in 3 hours 35 minutes and 21 seconds, making it the fastest (but not the first) marathon in space.

CROSSWORD

ACROSS

1. In 1961, Yuri Gagarin was the first man in _____
2. In 1969, Armstrong and Aldrin successfully completed the very first Moon _____
3. The name of Tereshkova's spacecraft
4. The name of the project that Sharman took part in
5. Helen Sharman was a British _____ and astronaut

DOWN

1. Yuri Gagarin was a Soviet _____ and cosmonaut
2. "That's one small step for man, one giant leap for mankind." were the first words spoken on the _____
3. Major Timothy Peake is a BritishArmy Air Corps _____ and European Space Agency Astronaut

WORDSEARCH

Q	G	P	I	L	O	T
K	A	H	G	P	S	E
A	G	L	J	U	H	R
R	A	H	G	S	A	E
M	R	N	Q	P	R	S
S	I	M	W	S	M	H
T	N	I	P	D	A	K
R	T	V	J	U	N	O
O	J	R	O	A	D	V
N	E	K	A	E	P	A
G	A	O	R	Z	X	I

GAGARIN
ARMSTRONG
TERESHKOVA
SHARMAN
PEAKE
JUNO
PILOT

MILESTONES

MILESTONES

Discover the milestones that have shaped, and are still shaping our knowledge of our world and all that surrounds us.

BOLDLY GO!

SPUTNIK 1
October 4th, 1957

The first satellite to be launched by the Soviet Union and successfully entered the Earth's orbit. Sputnik managed to orbit for three weeks before its batteries died. This event started the space race between the USA and Russia!

THE FIRST MAN IN SPACE
April 12th, 1961

Yuri Gagarin launched from Moscow in the Vostok 1 spacecraft. He orbited once around the world which lasted around 1 hour 29 minutes and landed at 10:55.

THE LUNAR LANDING
July 20th, 1969

The Apollo spacecraft launched from the Kennedy Space Centre at 9:32am heading towards the Moon. Aboard was Edwin E. Aldrin, Michael Collins and Neil Armstrong. Four days later, Armstrong manually landed the Lunar Landing Module (The Eagle) onto the Moons dusty surface. Armstrong descended the stairs and spoke the famous line. "That's one small step for man, one giant leap for mankind." They collected samples, took photographs and placed an American flag into the surface.

LAUNCH OF THE HUBBLE TELESCOPE
April 25th, 1990

Named after Edwin Powell Hubble, it is currently roughly 340 miles above Earth. Completing 15 orbits per day, it takes pictures of planets, stars and galaxies to send back to Earth, helping us to learn more about the universe.

VOYAGER 1

Voyager was launched in 1977 (along with Voyager 2). They were sent to explore the solar system. In August 2012, Voyager was the first man-made object to enter Interstellar space and is about 14 billion miles away. It continues to send information back to Earth! What a trooper!
It has been operating for 44 years (as of 2022) - 44 years with no break, not even bank holidays or Christmas!

CURIOSITY

Curiosity is a rover involved in NASA's Mars Science Laboratory mission. Launching in November 26, 2011 and landing in 2012, Curiosity sets out to investigate the planets conditions and if they're able to support life.
So far, its studies have found that the environments on Mars could have previously supported life!

QUIZ

1. Who was Yuri Gagarin?

_____

2. What was the name of the first satelite to launch successfully into the Earths orbit?

_____

3. What is the name of the telescope launched in 1990?

_____

4. Where is the rover, Curiosity?

_____

5. What's the name of the spacecraft that reached Interstellar space?

_____

6. Where did The Apollo spacecraft launch from?

_____

7. How long did Sputnik 1 orbit for?

_____

CROSSWORD

ACROSS

1. The name of the Spacecraft that entered Interstellar
2. Yuri Gagarin completed one _____ around the Earth
3. The name of the Lunar Landing Module Armstrong landed on the moon

DOWN

1. On August 2012, Voyager finally entered _____ space
2. In what month did Sputnik 1 launch?
3. Curiosity was looking for signs of _____

SPACE

SPACE

Ever wondered what amazing things are out there? What they're made of or what caused them? In this section, we will explore some of the many great things that live in our universe!

SUPER-KNOWER

THE MOON

The Moon is about 240,000 miles from Earth. It's full of craters caused by asteroids and comets hitting it. The Moon helps stabilize our planet and control our climate as well as our tides, causing them to be high or low depending on the gravitational pull known as tidal force.

BLACK HOLES

A black hole is an invisible force of inescapable gravitational pull from which not even light can leave! This can be caused by matter being squeezed into a small space from a giant star collapsing on itself. The only way to see a black hole is to witness its surroundings, e.g. stars and gases.
No one can say for sure what is inside a black hole, but it is thought to extend to infinity - **AND BEYOND!**

THE SUN

The Sun is a star (yellow dwarf) that is 4.5 billion years old, 93 million miles from Earth and is 100x wider. It is the largest object in our solar system and holds us all together with its large gravitational pull!
Because it is made of helium and hydrogen, its surface is not solid but instead made of burning hot plasma with the core reaching 27 million degrees Fahrenheit.

SUPERNOVA

A Supernova is a result of two possible changes in a stars core:
1. Dying star - when a star's core becomes too heavy the star will collapse and explode.
2. Binary star system - when a white dwarf obtains matter from its neighbouring star it will eventually become too heavy and explode.
The supernova only lasts a short time and ends with either a neutron star or a black hole.

The Milky Way

Our galaxy is held together by gravity and is made up of billions of stars, dust and gas. Astronomers believe that, because of some activity witnessed, e.g. vivid flares, the centre of the Milky Way's spiral shape could be home to a supermassive black hole!

Galaxies can collide!

Andromeda (Messier 31) is our nearest neighbouring galaxy which, astronomer's think, could have collided with possibly several galaxies already! Andromeda can be seen with the naked eye and is best observed in november!

WHICH IS WHICH?

Asteroid - An asteroid is a small rock that orbits the sun. Most asteroids are found in the asteroid belt between Jupiter and Mars.

Meteoroids - When two asteroids collide, small pieces can chip off. These are known as meteoroids.

Meteors - Sometimes meteoroids come into the Earth's atmosphere. When this happens, they start to burn up causing streaks of light - this becomes known as a 'shooting star'. This is caused by friction due to the speed in which the meteor is travelling.

Usually, they never survive the burn up, but if they do and hit the ground, they become known as 'meteorites'. A meteorite can cause damage to its surroundings (depending on its size).

Comets - Comets orbit the Sun. They are made of rock, frozen gas and dust. As the ice starts to vaporize, it can cause a visible tail and can be mistaken for a shooting star but is not!

SOLAR SYSTEM

SUN
Star at the centre of the solar system made of hydrogen and helium.

MARS
The 'Red Planet'. Named after the Roman God of War, its colour comes from rusty iron in the ground. It is thought to have had water and is also home to volcanoes (Mount Olympus) and ice caps. Mars takes 687 days to complete one orbit.

VENUS
Named after the Goddess of love and beauty and is one of the brightest objects in the sky.
Venus is also the hottest planet in our solar system), due to its thick atmosphere with surface temperatures reaching 475 degrees Celsius. It is also the only planet to spin clockwise around the sun and rains sulphuric acid (which evaporates in the heat before reaching the surface). Venus takes 225 days to complete one orbit.

MERCURY
Mercury is named after the Roman messenger of God and takes 88 days to complete one orbit.

EARTH
Our Home! The only planet, that we know of, that is home to living things. Earth is a Germanic name meaning 'the ground'.
It is known as an oblate spheroid, which means it is not quite spherical due to bulges in the middle. 71% of Earth is water and it is 4.543 billion years old!

NEPTUNE
Ice giant. Neptune is the only planet not visible from Earth with the naked eye. It takes 165 years to complete one orbit.

SATURN
A gas giant made predominantly of hydrogen and helium. The rings that surround Saturn are made of chunks of ice and rock. Saturn takes 29 years to complete one orbit.

JUPITER
The largest planet in our solar system and a gas giant! The famous 'Great Red Spot' is a giant storm bigger than Earth that has continued for hundreds of years. Jupiter's stripes are cold, windy clouds of ammonia and water, in an atmosphere of hydrogen and helium.

PLUTO
Dwarf planet in the Kuiper Belt. Pluto takes 248 years to complete one orbit. (Although, whether it is still considered a planet is debatable - poor Pluto!)

URANUS
Named after the Greek God of the Sky. Uranus take 84 years to complete one orbit.

MOON PHASE

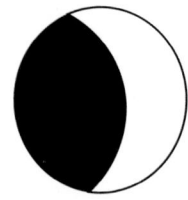

| New Moon | Waxing Cresent | First Quarter | Waxing Gibbous |

| Full Moon | Waning Gibbous | Last Quarter | Waning Cresent |

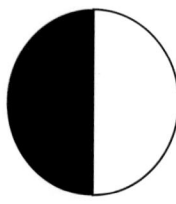

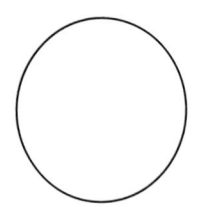

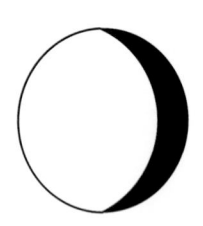

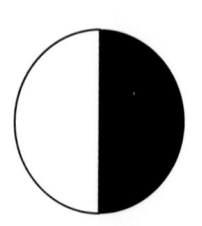

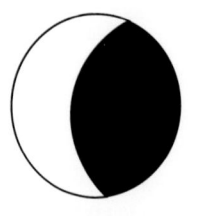

QUIZ

1. What is the name of the piece of rock known as a 'Shooting Star'?

   _____

2. Why can't we see Black Holes?

   _____

3. What are Comets made of?

   _____

4. What's the name of our closest galaxy?

   _____

5. What do astronomers believe is at the centre of our Galaxy, the Milky Way?

   _____

6. Why is the Moon full of craters?

   _____

7. What kind of star is the sun?

   _____

8. What are the two elements that make up the Sun?

   _____

STAR JOURNAL

OBSERVER: _____

DATE: _____

TIME: _____

LOCATION: _____

SKY CONDITION: _____

SEEING: _____

TRANSPARENCY: _____

I OBSERVED:

OBJECT: _____

TYPE: _____

CONSTELLATIONS: _____
_____
_____

TELESCOPE/ BINOCULARS/ NAKED EYE? _____

NOTES: _____
_____
_____
_____
_____
_____
_____

STAR JOURNAL

OBSERVER: _____

DATE: _____

TIME: _____

LOCATION: _____

SKY CONDITION: _____

SEEING: _____

TRANSPARENCY: _____

I OBSERVED:

OBJECT: _____

TYPE: _____

CONSTELLATIONS: _____

_____

_____

TELESCOPE/ BINOCULARS/ NAKED EYE? _____

NOTES: _____

_____

_____

_____

_____

_____

_____

STAR JOURNAL

OBSERVER: ⎯⎯⎯⎯⎯⎯⎯⎯⎯⎯⎯⎯⎯⎯⎯⎯⎯⎯⎯⎯⎯⎯⎯⎯⎯

DATE: ⎯⎯⎯⎯⎯⎯⎯⎯⎯⎯⎯⎯⎯⎯⎯⎯⎯⎯⎯⎯⎯⎯⎯⎯⎯⎯⎯⎯

TIME: ⎯⎯⎯⎯⎯⎯⎯⎯⎯⎯⎯⎯⎯⎯⎯⎯⎯⎯⎯⎯⎯⎯⎯⎯⎯⎯⎯⎯

LOCATION: ⎯⎯⎯⎯⎯⎯⎯⎯⎯⎯⎯⎯⎯⎯⎯⎯⎯⎯⎯⎯⎯⎯⎯⎯

SKY CONDITION: ⎯⎯⎯⎯⎯⎯⎯⎯⎯⎯⎯⎯⎯⎯⎯⎯⎯⎯⎯

SEEING: ⎯⎯⎯⎯⎯⎯⎯⎯⎯⎯⎯⎯⎯⎯⎯⎯⎯⎯⎯⎯⎯⎯⎯⎯

TRANSPARENCY: ⎯⎯⎯⎯⎯⎯⎯⎯⎯⎯⎯⎯⎯⎯⎯⎯⎯⎯⎯

I OBSERVED:

OBJECT: ⎯⎯⎯⎯⎯⎯⎯⎯⎯⎯⎯⎯⎯⎯⎯⎯⎯⎯⎯⎯⎯⎯⎯⎯

TYPE: ⎯⎯⎯⎯⎯⎯⎯⎯⎯⎯⎯⎯⎯⎯⎯⎯⎯⎯⎯⎯⎯⎯⎯⎯⎯

CONSTELLATIONS: ⎯⎯⎯⎯⎯⎯⎯⎯⎯⎯⎯⎯⎯⎯⎯⎯

TELESCOPE/ BINOCULARS/ NAKED EYE? ⎯⎯⎯⎯

NOTES: ⎯⎯⎯⎯⎯⎯⎯⎯⎯⎯⎯⎯⎯⎯⎯⎯⎯⎯⎯⎯⎯⎯⎯⎯

Quiz Answers:

Page 28 crossword:

Answers: Space, Landing, Vostok, Juno, Chemist
Answers: Pilot, Moon, Officer

Page 34, 35

Answers:

1. The first man in space
2. Sputnik 1
3. The Hubble
4. Mars
5. Voyager 1
6. Kennedy Space Centre
7. 3 weeks

Answers:

1. Voyager
2. Orbit
3. Eagle

1. Interstellar
2. October
3. Life

Page 43

Answers:

1. Meteors
2. They are invisible
3. Ice and dust
4. Andomeda
5. Black hole
6. Because it is being hit by asteroids and comets
7. Yellow dwarf
8. Hydrogen and helium

MOON JOURNAL

Fill out your Moon Journal every night for a month to track all the phases of the Moon!

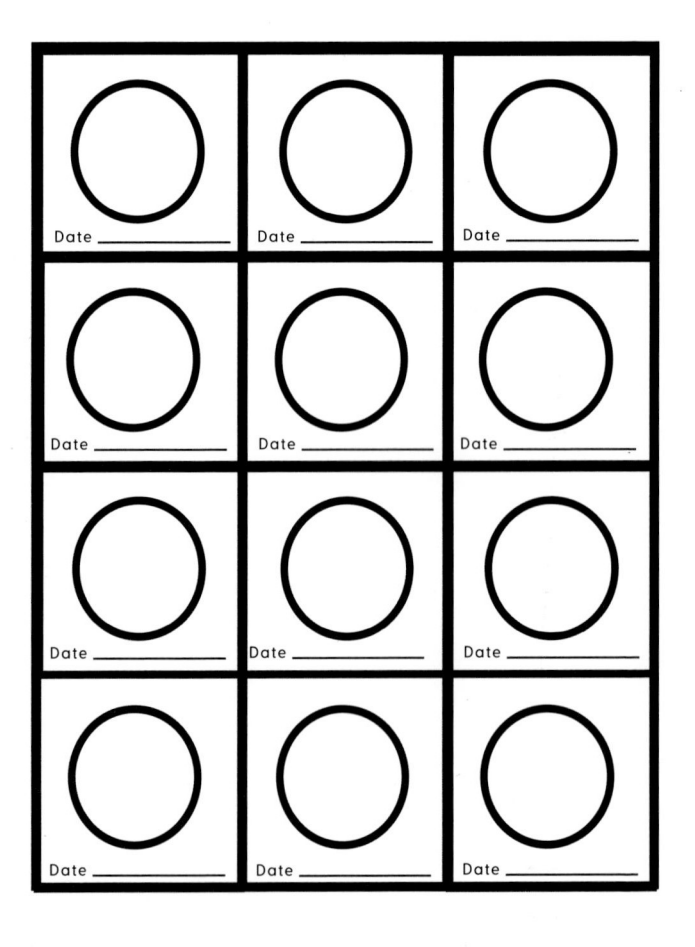

Date _____	Date _____	Date _____
Date _____	Date _____	Date _____
Date _____	Date _____	Date _____
Date _____	Date _____	Date _____

Date started _____